THE STRAND OF HAIR
AMOY
MY AUTOBIOGRAPHY

BOOK ONE

Dr. Amoy D. Baker Ph.D.

Copyright © 2024 Dr. Amoy D. Baker

All rights reserved. No part of this publication may be reproduced, distributed, or transmitted in any form or by any means, including photocopying, recording, or other electronic or mechanical methods, without the prior written permission of the publisher, except in the case of brief quotations embodied in critical reviews and certain other noncommercial uses permitted by copyright law.

DEDICATION

I dedicate this book as my legacy of truth and strength to my husband and my three sons. I strive to show them that they are stronger than they think. Struggles will come, but when they do, use them to build your strength. If you must cry, then cry. Whatever you do, don't give up. Don't throw in the towel; use it to wipe your tears and keep going. I live by Philippians 4:13: "I can do all things through Christ who strengthens me."

All things are possible if you only believe. — Mark 9:23

CONTENTS

My Abstract - This Is My Truth 1

Introduction 3

Chapter 1 – My Perception of It All 5

Chapter 2 – Abused and Confused 9

Chapter 3 – Falsely Beaten 15

Chapter 4 – Surprise Move 17

Chapter 5 – Meeting My Mother 19

Chapter 6 – Back and Forth 23

Chapter 7 – The Tent Meeting PS. 27:10 27

Chapter 8 – The Visit 33

Chapter 9 – New Family 35

Chapter 10 – Legal Adoption 37

Chapter 11 – The Journey 39

Chapter 12 – Travel to Canada and America 47

Chapter 13 – The Beginning Of The New Journey 53

Chapter 14 – Keep It Pushing 57

Chapter 15 – Where Do I Go From Here? 61

About the Author 65

MY ABSTRACT
THIS IS MY TRUTH

One day I opened my eyes and realized that I was a 6-year-old girl and that I lived in a world that was not normal. This was 1981 in a big city called Kingston, Jamaica, West Indies.

It was a world where everything that surrounded me and everything I was involved in seemed normal. This was the only world I knew—a world where abuse was normal, where beatings were normal, where verbal abuse was normal, and where physical and sexual abuse was normal. In this world, my voice did not matter, my emotions meant nothing, and I was not allowed to have feelings. This was especially true for a small child with no mother or father to protect them in a third-world country. This world was dark, lonely, painful, draining, weakening, blinding, and sad.

Time went by so fast, and then I was grown up. I didn't know where I was, I didn't know where I came from, and I didn't know where I was going. I opened my eyes one day and realized that my world had changed, or maybe I had changed through some strange human metamorphosis. Suddenly, everything seemed different, and I was not familiar with this new experience. I began to reflect on what was normal to me, and that's where I found my strength—that was my safe place. I found safety in loneliness, in sadness, in fear, and I did not try to find joy in anything other than what seemed normal to me.

Changes began to happen that I did not plan for, like being in a world where people spoke to me as if I were human. People were smiling and talking and behaving as if happiness was good, but I did not understand what was happening around me. I saw mothers and fathers with their children, playing and being nice, which was very abnormal for me to see. Why should I conform to this new world? What does it feel like to smile and laugh as they do? Is there really such a thing as love, joy, and happiness? I actually had feelings—they moved along my body like crawling insects whenever things happened. I didn't realize that I was allowed to feel. Wow, what a strange world. The saying is true: there really is a light at the end of the tunnel, and time will tell it in this story.

INTRODUCTION

I am writing this story to inspire my generation to understand that it is okay to seek redemption. In my Gen X, men and women were taught to endure in silence. We lived by the phrases, "Speak when you are spoken to" and "Answer when you are called." Questions were discouraged, and opinions were unwelcome. We ate what we were given, or we did not eat at all.

The control that someone had over our minds could easily manipulate us. This manipulation could create a false sense of love and acceptance, blinding us from seeing who we really were and hindering us from becoming our best selves. Although some level of discipline is necessary for children, these instructions and disciplines were often misused for the satisfaction and pleasure of certain guardians.

I am writing this book in honor of, and with love and inspiration from, my husband and my three sons. This book is meant to encourage all my friends and my community to understand the story and the reasons behind why I am, "The Strand of Hair."

I
MY PERCEPTION OF IT ALL

As the story was told to me when I was a small child, I listened with an open but confused mind. At the age of six, I began to realize that I existed, that I was a little girl, and that my life was very different from the people around me. I started to ask questions, which caused more trouble for me than I realized. I noticed children with their families and saw that they had mothers, fathers, and people who seemed to care for them. I was curious. By the time I became curious about my own family, I realized that I was living with my aunt. I looked around and noticed that I had no mother or father. I started to ask my friends about their moms and dads. They explained to me that they had parents, but some did not. Some mentioned that their fathers and mothers were either gone or dead. Others said they had family members who cared for them lovingly. There were children who stayed with their grandparents, aunts, uncles, and friends and were not being treated the way I was, which confused me even more. How could they stay with people who were not even related and still receive love? This was intriguing to me, so I decided to ask my aunt about my mother and father. The moment I opened my mouth to ask, I wished I never had.

My aunt lived in one of the biggest towns in our parish. It was a beautiful two-story home with a restaurant and bar on the top floor. This bar had seven toilets for both males and females. In the restaurant area, there were tables and chairs and lots of windows. She also had a very pretty kitchen with two big sinks and lots of dishes. There was a big backyard with lots of big trees, all fenced in. I was only six when I realized I was living with this aunt, and to me, this was the biggest house in the world. Every day, there were lots and lots of people coming in and out to eat, drink, listen to music, and make a lot of noise. I also remembered she had two rooms on the side of the house. People would come in and out of those rooms day and night. I wasn't sure what was going on because I had to stay focused on my duties so that I wouldn't get in trouble and lose my meal for the day.

My Duties

I was awakened each morning by loud sounds and yelling, cursing, and things being thrown at me to get out of bed. My first duty was to make up my bedding, sweep and mop the floors in my room area, then dust each window in the area where I slept. I then needed to clean all seven toilets in the restrooms for the customers and sweep and mop those floors as well. There were body fluids all around the toilets and floors, which were often hard for me to clean. I was small, so I couldn't reach the corners most of the time. I would climb on different things trying to get inside and behind the toilet, but I just couldn't reach—I was too short. I also had to rake, sweep, pick up, and straighten the yard each morning before any customers showed up for lunch. Most days, I just couldn't get it all done on time since they started coming around 12 pm. Once I finished in the bathrooms and outside in the yard, she inspected them. Most of the time, I could hear her yelling, screaming, and calling me names in our native language, Patois. She would say things like, "You are dirty, nasty, good for nothing, little brute, little shit," and I wasn't getting anything to eat until I cleaned it right. As I listened and swept the yard with hunger, pain, sadness, and frustration, I just wanted to die. Most days, I would be in the restrooms cleaning as people came in and out to use them. I couldn't leave until my aunt was satisfied. After a while, I had severe sores and bumps all over my hands, face, and body from the toilets I cleaned each day. Some days, the men who came in to use the restrooms would see me and try to talk to me to make me feel better. People would sneak food to me because they saw I was hungry. Sometimes, they would mention to her to let me eat, but she would get very angry and tell them to mind their own business. Some of the same men would say comforting words and ask me to come near them so they could hug me.

Most of these men would touch my private area with their fingers, and my bottom would be so sore and painful. Some days, I couldn't urinate because of the burning and pain. One morning, I tried to show my aunt the sores and let her know I was feeling sick and that I wasn't strong enough to clean that day. She lifted her arm and slapped me so hard that three of my teeth came out. She began screaming at me, saying I was nasty and it was all my fault and if I ever told anybody about these things, she would kill me. During this moment, she began to beat me with a piece of stick that she had in her room and shoved me out to go and start my chores. This treatment went on for about two years that I can remember. I can't remember anything before that, so you can imagine.

I remember, I was in the yard sweeping and crying. Crying because my body was so sore and I was tired and weak. As I swept close to the fence, I heard a noise, scratching on the other side of the fence. I stopped for a quick moment to take a peek. It was a little boy a little older than I was. He was trying to get my attention to come to the fence so that he could talk to me. As I approached, he smiled and slid a small spoon through the fence with some peanut butter on it for me to eat. He asked if I was okay and said his name was Junior. I was very happy to meet him but scared that my aunt would see me talking to him, so I ate it and went back to sweeping. He quickly called me back and pushed the water hose through the fence for me to take a drink. After that day, we became friends until he moved away, and I never saw him again.

The abuse continued for a long while after my friend left, but I kept going to the fence every day as if he were there talking to me. There was a farmer's market nearby where everyone knew my aunt, and they all seemed to like her. One morning after she left the house, I stopped working and went down to the market to get food. One of her friends saw me and began to ask me questions about the sores and what was going on to contribute to the way I looked at the time. She called out to another friend to take a look at my sores and my condition. I started to cry and asked them not to tell her that I came outside or to say that I told them anything. It must have been about two weeks later—I had no concept of time, so I am not sure how long it was—I was in the yard sweeping when I heard people fussing and arguing. Suddenly, the back door swung open, and a woman came down to me and picked me up with tears in her eyes and took me away. It was another one of my aunts, but I didn't know it at the time.

2
ABUSED AND CONFUSED

It was a bright, sunny morning when I woke up at my new aunt's home. I jumped up, thinking I was late for my chores and would get in trouble. I looked around, noticing no one was screaming or throwing things at me - the house was silent. I felt scared because I wasn't used to that.

My new aunt came to my room and said hi. I quivered with fear, squeezing myself into the corner because I thought she would beat me for something. My aunt quickly grabbed and held me, telling me it was all over and I didn't have to be afraid anymore. She cried, saying she would take care of me because I was her brother's child. She told me she loved me and wished my father had left me with her in the first place. That was the first time I had ever heard my father mentioned. I didn't want to ask questions, afraid of what might happen if I did.

My aunt made me breakfast, and for the first time I could remember, I was able to eat a full meal before doing my chores. I was still scared, feeling like I was being set up for something bad. No one had ever been this nice without wanting to hurt me, so I didn't trust her. I was prepared for anything. I didn't understand why she was so kind or what she might want from me in return. So many questions raced through my mind. I was unsure, nervous, frightened and lost - something didn't feel right. I just didn't understand how someone could be so nice to me.

She noticed the sores on my body and began asking about them. I was terrified to tell her what was going on because I didn't want another beating for talking about it. But she comforted me until I could share a little. She examined my body, seeing how the sores had spread. She cried, talking to me about what she saw, then immediately got dressed and took me to the doctor. She continued caring for me until all the sores went away and I felt better physically. I was so happy and felt loved, if only for a time.

Being so young, I had little concept of time passing. I'll estimate about two months after starting to feel better, things changed. Of course, like any household, everyone had duties, which was no problem since that's what I was used to. Every morning I got up, made my bed and straightened the areas I was told, with ease. No extra toilets to clean, no yard to sweep, no old men to touch me, and best of all, I got to eat without working for food. I began attending a small school not too far from the house. I remember walking because there were no buses or cars, but it was okay.

I never wanted friends because I didn't know how to be one, so I kept to myself. Late one afternoon coming from school, I walked alone. There were other kids with friends and families, usually on the other side of the road. But that day it seemed like not many were out walking.

Up ahead, I saw a couple boys, maybe a little older than me, sitting on the side of the road. By this time, I believe I was about seven because I knew I had a birthday, just not the day, year or month.

As I got closer, the boys began throwing rocks at me, calling me strange names. They came up, pushing me and pulling at the books in my hands. Now as an adult, I realize they must have been around 10 to 12 years old. One boy snatched me to the ground, squeezing my breasts until it hurt. I was fighting and kicking as much as I could. I managed to get up and tried to run away, but they grabbed me again, pulling me into an empty nearby building. They began tearing off my underwear, pushing and tugging at my private area as I screamed.

Suddenly, I heard a lady calling out, "Hello! Who's in there? Who's making that noise? What's going on?" The boys, scared, jumped up and ran off to the other side of the building. The lady had to help me climb up the slight hill out of the building. I told her what happened and where I lived, so she took me home. When I got there, I didn't say anything at first because I was scared and terrified I would be blamed.

My aunt had four children living there too, and they were all home, but I didn't tell anyone. I went to clean up, pull myself together so I could do my afternoon chores and homework. Later that night, I was near my aunt's room. I decided to tell her what happened because after all, she had shown me so much love and care.

But as I spoke to her, she became very upset, yelling at me, "What did you do to the boys? Where are your panties? Why don't you have pants on?" And so on. She took a belt from nearby pants and began beating me intensely. I was in shock at what was happening - confused, ashamed of myself, wanting to die right then. What did I do? I must be a really bad person. No one likes me, I don't deserve love, I hated myself and deserved to die. These were my thoughts as I went numb during the beating. Back to my comfort zone of not understanding anything.

All the children were home, so they heard and saw the whole thing. She told everyone I was being "fast" and wanting to have sex and be grown. She completely ignored my cry for help.

After that day, I decided I would never share anything with anyone ever again, no matter what happened to me. If I died, then so be it - the world would be fine without me. Those were my thoughts.

Now as an adult, I understand a clear message was sent to anyone who desired to take advantage of me. Not long after that beating, I turned eight. I knew my birthday because someone close had the same one, and they told me it was mine too - I was happy to find that out.

One of my male cousins, one of my aunt's sons, called me to his room to do a chore. I thought nothing of it since I always did things for them. This day, he came up to me and exposed himself, then started rubbing himself on me. Everything from my first aunt's situation flashed in my head. What do I do now? Fight him? Scream? Would it even matter what I did? At this point I was worthless, belonged to no one, and deserved whatever I got. I didn't care anymore what anyone did to me.

He put his hands in my panties and began hurting me, then sexually abused me until I bled profusely. We were home alone at the time, and he was the oldest boy, so I was terrified and didn't tell anyone. For a very long time I was extremely swollen and in pain, and even through that, he would constantly touch me and threaten me never to say anything.

There was another brother, the second of her three sons, who didn't know this was going on. He seemed their mother's favorite, so whatever he said mattered. This was the son mainly left in charge of overseeing me and ensuring I did all my duties correctly. I couldn't go outside to play or talk to anyone without his permission. None of my chores were complete to his mother's satisfaction unless he said so.

While the sexual abuse continued with the first son, this second son decided to do the same. He would actually beat me if I didn't do what he said sexually. Whenever he beat me, he would lie, saying I didn't want to do my chores properly, which was why he beat me. So now I was back to square one emotionally and mentally.

There were days I attempted to tell my aunt he was lying, but then she would beat me even more because she said I was calling her son a liar.

This aunt also owned a bar away from the house. She would leave to work there all day and sometimes come home drunk. Whenever she came home and her son told her I didn't do my chores properly, I would get a beating and then her verbal abuse began. She would say I was good for nothing, worthless, dirty - she hated me like poison and I'd be just like my good-for-nothing father. Sounds familiar?

So what was I supposed to think as a little girl in this world? Since whenever I told the truth I got beaten and abused, why should I tell the truth about anything since it didn't matter? So I became defiant, disobedient, rude, bitter and sad. After all, that's how they all saw me. I began to lie about every and anything I could think of, and guess what? They believed all the lies. Strange, very strange.

3

FALSELY BEATEN

This part of my 7-year-old life stands out to me, highlighting the complexities of people and the world around me. My impression of people was very mixed and confusing. I tried to find my place in this world, to see where I fit in, but I couldn't find any. The abuse continued for a while from the brothers and my aunt. I remember a particular day when I came home from school and saw that dinner was ready. The brother in charge of making sure my chores were done told me to do the dishes, sweep the living room, and then do my homework. I did everything he asked and then fell asleep on the couch.

I'm not sure how long I slept, but I was awakened by beatings and yelling from my aunt. I jumped up in fear and distress as the beating continued. I asked over and over, "What did I do wrong?" She did not answer but just kept beating me. I got hit in my eyes, head, back—everywhere. Finally, I got away and slid under the bed to hide from her. She walked away and said she had something for me. She came back and pulled me by the leg from under the bed. Instead of a belt, she now had a metal ruler in her hand. She began to beat my head with the ruler over and over again. Suddenly, I felt a warm flow going down my face and noticed it was blood everywhere. She had beaten my head until I began to bleed. I was extremely afraid and really thought I was going to die this time. One of my cousins, a girl, finally asked her to stop. She did not listen; she just kept beating me and saying I deserved everything I got. She then threw the ruler down and walked away.

That very same night, the cousin who asked her to stop beating me came to talk to me. She seemed very sad for me and wanted me to feel better. I asked her, "What did I do wrong? Why did she beat me this way?" My cousin said she did not know because my aunt did not say. My aunt only kept cursing, fussing, and yelling profanities, saying that she hated me. My cousin left after she helped clean the blood from my head and face. She went to tell my aunt that I needed to go to the hospital. I can't remember if I even went, but I think I did. I do remember my aunt threatening me not to tell anyone how I got the injury and to say I fell.

Later that night, my cousin informed me that my aunt said I stole chicken from the meal that was cooked that day. I was shocked because I had no idea what she was talking about. I was too afraid of her and knew I would never have done anything like that. I never touched the pot on the stove; I never stole anything from the kitchen. I did the dishes, cleaned up, did my homework, and then fell asleep on the couch—that's all. I tried to ask my cousin to tell her mom that I did not do it, but she was afraid as well and did not want to get in trouble for trying to defend me. So, the sexual and physical abuse continued for a while—many years, at least it seemed to me like it was years upon years.

4

SURPRISE MOVE

One day after school, my aunt told me to pack my bags and get ready to go. Confused and afraid, I complied silently. Outside, a car was waiting, its engine humming softly. As we drove, my aunt's anger boiled over, her tirade against my father filling the air. In our native Jamacan language, patois (pronounced as pa·twuh), she called me worthless, a liar, and unwanted. The driver remained silent, his gaze fixed ahead, as I listened in silence, feeling the weight of her words.

We arrived at a marketplace nestled in the mountains, a place unfamiliar to me. Uncertainty gnawed at me as we unloaded my bags. Passing through a broken gate, I found myself in a yard where children played. My aunt approached a woman who emerged from the house, and they began to talk. It was then I discovered that this woman was the sister of my biological mother.

Imagine being an 8 ½ to 9-year-old girl, hearing this revelation. Despite my age, I felt small, lost, and terrified, like a tiny mouse in a vast, confusing world.

The Baby Story:

The conversation turned ugly, curses flying through the air. My aunt hurled my belongings into the yard before storming off, leaving me behind. The children, sensing something amiss, watched with concern. My new aunt, though uncertain, showed me love and comfort, offering me solace in her home. She shared a shocking revelation: I was her little sister's child, born during a tumultuous time.

My mother was just 13 when she became pregnant, and my grandmother demanded she get rid of the baby. Chemicals meant to induce abortion failed, and at four months old, my mother and aunt decided to give me to my father to raise. They went to his house, but he was gone, so they asked my aunt to care for me until he returned. However, weeks later, when my mother came to retrieve me, I was nowhere to be found. The search for me lasted years, hindered by misinformation and familial estrangement.

The story my new aunt told conflicted with what I had been told before. My previous aunt claimed my mother had abandoned me in a cardboard box on a doorstep. It was a bizarre tale, told with disgust, but now, my new aunt insisted that wasn't the truth. She assured me they had never stopped looking for me, and after a brief stay, she contacted my mother, informing her of our meeting.

The prospect of meeting my mother filled me with fear. What would this reunion bring?

5

MEETING MY MOTHER

The day finally came for me to travel a long distance to meet my mother for the first time. I was terrified. What if she didn't want me? What if she didn't like me? What if I didn't like her? What if she said she didn't want me? What if she had other children who didn't want me? Was she mean like my aunts? What if I wasn't good enough? So many questions raced through my mind. I was scared, nervous and afraid, but my aunt did her best to comfort me until we arrived. I felt like a tumbleweed, blown here and there, lost in the wind.

After we arrived at the bus station, we had to walk a long way, maybe around four miles now that I think about it. Remember, I was little, so I had no concept of time or distance, but it felt like 10,000 miles. We had to carry all my bags, with the hope that I would get to stay. My aunt couldn't keep me because she had her own children and family situation. When we finally arrived at my mother's house, I saw plenty of children playing outside. When they saw me, they ran up, bombarding me with questions. "Are you my sister? Are you going to live with us?" It was overwhelming, so I just walked straight ahead, unable to answer.

We got to the door and a woman came out, greeting my aunt joyfully, glad to see her sister. She looked at me and cried out, "My daughter!" She said, "Hold on, let me look at you. I want to see if you have a certain mark." It was getting dark in that rural area, so she brought a lamp close to my face to check for a black mole on my lip. She began weeping loudly, "This is my daughter! This is my lost baby! She is really my daughter! Oh my God!"

She cried and cried, thanking my aunt for bringing her baby back. She tried asking me questions, but it was too much. I was scared, shivering as I cried on her shoulders, unsure what would come next. So I just sat on the ground, trying to make sense of it all. "Are all these children my family?" I asked. One of the girls tried wiping tears from her eyes, reassuring me, "Don't cry, I'm your sister and you can stay here with us." I didn't know how to feel. The whole scene spun around me as I cried, overwhelmed by mixed emotions. You can imagine my brain just stopped working - my mind froze as a rushing force of feelings and emotions hit me like a hurricane.

After everything calmed down, she offered me food and drink, showing me where I would sleep that night until she could sort out living arrangements.

Now that I think about it, she herself didn't have much. If I remember correctly, she had five or six children with her at the time, so I would have been the seventh, but the firstborn of them all. I was the first to be born, but the last to come home.

It was time for my aunt to go, as it was getting extremely late and the buses would stop running soon. As she left, I felt that serious pain of abandonment once again in such a short period. I had just left one abusive aunt, only to experience similar treatment from another. I just wanted someone to take all this pain away.

Not long after, I was packed up and shipped off to yet another unknown family in an unknown place. And now, left with these people who claimed to be family and wanted to be part of my life.

I stayed with my mother and siblings before the trouble began. Usually my siblings and I would need to fetch water for household use. This particular evening, as we approached the house after getting our usual bucket of water, we heard a lot of yelling and screaming - it was my mother and stepfather, who lived with all of us, fighting.

As I drew closer, I noticed clothes strewn all over the yard. I was shocked to see they all belonged to me. My mouth dropped open, I dropped the water bucket and ran towards the house crying, "What's wrong?" My mother approached me, grabbing my shirt and asking frantically, "Did you let him touch you?" I immediately responded, "No no! He didn't touch me!" But she kept yelling, clearly very upset. I was scared, confused, not understanding what was happening. I heard my stepfather begging and pleading for her to believe he didn't touch me. I knew for certain he was telling the truth.

Even now as an adult, I stand by that truth. My stepfather did not touch me inappropriately. First, as a small child I was afraid of him because he only had one arm. As a little girl, I was extremely scared of that lone arm, so if he ever came near me, everyone in the house would have known. Amid my mother's yelling, I heard her say one of my sisters gave her that false information. The father in heaven knew it was a lie. For some strange reason, my sister made up that lie, and now I was being thrown out on the street.

My mother told me she didn't want me and that I was to go back where I came from. She said I could never be her daughter, that I was disgusting for letting him touch me. She didn't want to hear it - she didn't want me in her house and wanted me gone as soon as possible. One sibling helped gather my clothes into a bag, then helped carry them to the side of the road. There were some cucumbers growing there, so I picked a few, knowing I wouldn't have anything else to eat. She mentioned already sending a friend to call my aunt to come get me, but didn't know when they were coming. She just needed me out of her sight so her life could go back to normal.

She yelled at me, "Go away!"

6

BACK AND FORTH

After a while, the bus came and my aunt got off, walking the distance to pick me up. When she saw me, she cried, saying, "I don't know what I'm going to do because you cannot stay here with me." I ended up staying there with her for about two weeks. During that time, I never heard from my mother or had any mention of her. At first, my aunt was trying to discuss with her about keeping me, but it just wasn't working out.

One evening, my aunt came to me and said she had a friend - an older lady who lived alone with no children of her own. She mentioned this lady agreed for me to stay with her for a period of time. But she made it clear I would have chores and other responsibilities to pull my weight for staying there. I was happy and sad at the same time. Happy I had somewhere to go, and that the lady had no children, so I didn't have to worry about not being accepted. Sad to be moving again. My aunt took me to meet the lady. It was a very tiny house where the toilet, bed and kitchen were all in one small room. But it was okay with me because I had somewhere to lay my head, and it was a small area, so not much to clean.

One night, I was awoken by a lot of noise coming from the ceiling. I opened my eyes, trying to look around without turning on the light since she was sleeping. I heard something fall and scurry across the floor. I jumped up to see what it was, and all I could see were a bunch of red eyes darting around. I was terrified! I started screaming. I saw some very big, giant rats that I had never seen before. I cried and cried, not wanting to stay there. I ran outside and sat under a mango tree, unable to sleep the rest of the night out of fear. I had nowhere to go and no way to contact my aunt.

I stayed outside that whole night. The next morning, the lady took me to the bus stop and told the driver where to take me. When I arrived at my aunt's (my mom's sister), she was very surprised to see me. She searched and searched to find another friend who could keep me, but had a hard time.

In the meantime, I would stay with neighbors some days. Other days I would stay outside by the tree. I would eat from the trash if I could find any scraps, not wanting my aunt to feed me too when she had her own family - there just wasn't enough food. Eventually, somehow I ended up back at my second aunt's - the one with the sexually abusive sons - and stayed with her for a short time before the abuse started again.

This time I tried to tell her about one son's behavior, and that was a big mistake. She grabbed a nearby broom and beat me until it was broken, then grabbed something else, beating me so badly that we ended up outside by the front gate. My left knee was so swollen, and I was limping, so a neighbor came over and pulled me away from her. She had beaten my knee out of its socket.

I stayed at the neighbor's house that night. The next day, she took me back to my mom's sister, so now she had to start over trying to find somewhere else for me to stay. After weeks of searching, she finally did.

There was a lady about 10 miles from where my mom lived. She had adult children and two girls around my age. The lady had plenty of kids but didn't seem to mind having me there. The girls and I became very close, and this was one of the best situations I had been in. I still had plenty of chores, which was fine since I was used to it and knew it was expected of me.

I was able to start going back to school, and by this time, I was about 10 years old. I believe I stayed with this family for about two years, though since I was still young with little concept of time, it may have been a little shorter.

7

THE TENT MEETING PS. 27:10

I came home from school one day to find one of the girls very excited about some exciting news in our small town community. Since this was a rural area, there weren't too many events happening. In her excitement, she explained that a church from America was coming to have a big tent revival in our community. She wanted me to go just for fun, explaining that a lot of Americans would be there, along with people from our town and surrounding areas. I became excited and decided to go with her, of course having to walk about 2 miles, but that was okay – it would be fun.

The revival wasn't set to start for two weeks, but the anticipation kept us excited. After much waiting, the day finally came. We were told it would begin at 7pm. Since it was evening, we had to ensure all our chores were complete before we could go, so we got them done very early and headed down the road. By the time we arrived at the tent, they had already started. The tent was massive, with rows and rows of chairs surrounded by people.

It was so exciting to see such a large crowd, including white Americans. Listening to the lively worship with singing, drums and keyboard music sounded amazing. As we clapped, sang and danced for Jesus, I felt free, happy – like this was a good place for me. Everyone was very friendly and nice, giving hugs, laughing, shaking hands and showing so much love. I didn't want that night to end, but it was okay because we had four more nights since it was a one-week revival.

During that revival week, I saw so many miracles that I had never witnessed before. I saw a blind man regain his sight, a man with a short leg have his limb restored to full length, and many other amazing miracles that gave me hope. At first I was scared and uncertain about what I was seeing, but after the third miracle, I became filled with hope that maybe a miracle could happen for me too.

On the last night, which I remember was a Friday, I didn't want to go to school that day because I was anticipating the final revival service and didn't want to be late. I got home and did my chores very early, but didn't want to eat dinner – I was too excited. I wanted to get down to the tent early to be one of the first ones there. I waited for my friend, but she took a long time getting home even though we went to the same school but caught different buses. I waited for her as long as I could, then left on the journey alone.

When I arrived, there was no one there yet, but eventually the musicians showed up. I watched as they set up the instruments and checked the mics – oh boy, I was so excited, I could hardly wait! I believe I was at least two hours early because I had to wait a long time before people began showing up. Finally, everyone started arriving and the preachers came. All the seats filled up and praise and worship began.

Even though I was the first one there, I sat in the back because I was scared and afraid of the preachers noticing me. The night before, they had pointed people out, calling them to the front, and I didn't want to be called on. The preacher that night preached on Psalm 27, but the verse that stuck out most to me was verse 10: "When your father and your mother forsake you, the Lord will take you up." Out of everything said, that was the verse that resonated with me. I wanted to be taken up, I didn't want to be forsaken anymore.

Now I had this desire to go up front to sit, but there were no seats available. After wrestling with that for a few moments, I felt freed again. I began thinking to myself – every time someone picked me up, they just put me back down. Every time someone rescued me, they threw me back out on the street. How would I know this "Lord" would really take me up? What if this whole thing was a lie, just false hope that would get me thrown away again? Maybe this God, if he's a man, would want to abuse me too. He may want to use me and lay on me. I really wanted to be loved.

The pastor then began calling for people to come to the front if they wanted him to pray for them. "If you believe Jesus is your Lord and Savior and you want to be saved, come up to Jesus!" he urged. I didn't know if I believed him, and I didn't even know if I could be saved. I just wanted someone to love me, care for me, and never give up on me again. But what was I thinking? I was dreaming – this could never happen to me. I'm not good enough. Who would want to take in a liar, a hateful, ugly mess like me? I should stop dreaming and just go back up the hill to the house. They were getting ready to close out anyway, so I might as well go home. It was nice while it lasted, and I'll come back again.

I was going to leave when the pastor said out loud, "You, young lady!" He yelled it, and everyone turned to look, trying to figure out who he was referring to since we had all turned around, including me. I was wearing a green shirt that day, but at the time didn't think about what I had on. The pastor clarified, "The young lady in the green!" The process of elimination began – I was wearing green, but surely he couldn't be talking to me, there's no way. After a short moment, everyone realized he was calling me, and they started pulling at me to go up front. My heart was pounding, everyone was staring at me, and I felt like I had done something wrong. That night, my friend had come after I got there, but then she left - I don't know where she went, but she had never left me alone there before, so I was concerned.

With fear and trembling, I slowly walked to the front of the tent in front of all the pastors and people staring. I was so scared and embarrassed, unsure if I was in trouble for something I had done or how I looked. The pastor began comforting me, telling me not to be afraid, that everything was okay - he just wanted to talk to me. He asked a few questions like if I was there with someone, who my parents were, if I lived in the area, my name and age. I don't even remember if I answered any of those. I just didn't know why he wanted to single me out of all people there. He asked if it was okay for him to pray for me. I agreed yes, but reluctantly, as I had never had anyone pray for me before.

He began praying over me fervently, while my eyes were wide open because I didn't trust him or anyone around me. In my mind, I thought something bad was about to happen. When he stopped praying, he said, "I don't know where you are or where you come from, but the Lord wants you to know that he loves you." I looked up at him with eyes full of fear and confusion, thinking how could he love me when he doesn't even know me? Because if you knew me, he wouldn't love me. If the Lord hears all the horrible things my family has said about me, he wouldn't love me, because I don't love myself because of all the terrible things I know about myself. So I was very confused, not understanding what was going on.

Right before I walked away, he said to me, "The Lord is going to give you a family of your own that will love you and care for you one day. Just remember he's watching over you and he loves you." I didn't know what to make of any of it.

8
THE VISIT

Two days after the revival, I was on my way home from school when my friend eagerly approached me at the bus stop. She was bursting with excitement, telling me there was a visitor at our house for me. Confused, I asked her who it was and what they wanted. She replied, "It's that pastor man from the church." I was taken aback; I hadn't been thinking about any pastor or church. Skeptical, I laughed, thinking she was pulling my leg. However, she insisted it was true. As we approached the house, I saw a white van parked outside—something unusual, as nobody in our household drove. Nervously, I walked up to the gate and spotted the two men my friend had mentioned: the pastors.

Both men greeted me warmly, but I couldn't help feeling apprehensive. I asked if I had done something wrong and if I was in trouble. Tearfully, I apologized, pledging not to do whatever it was again. They assured me I had done nothing wrong and that they were there to talk to me about something good. The black pastor, the same one who had told me Jesus loved me at the tent meeting, explained that they had spoken to the lady I was staying with and learned my address from someone in the community.

He said Jesus had directed him to find me and that he and his wife wanted to offer me the love promised by Jesus.

I was dumbfounded. I couldn't comprehend what was happening and found it hard to believe them. I walked away to speak to the lady I was staying with, seeking reassurance. She explained that the pastors couldn't have children and had been praying for a baby girl. When they saw me, they believed I was the answer to their prayers. Confused, I pointed out that I wasn't a baby. However, she reassured me, explaining that they considered me the child they had been praying for.

I still didn't fully understand and asked the pastor to leave until his wife felt better and could talk to me. He agreed, expressing his desire for me to be happy and promising to return. He waved goodbye and left with his brother in the white van. For the next week, I remained silent, trying to process everything. I couldn't shake the feeling that this was another attempt to get rid of me. However, a week later, the pastors returned, this time with just the wife. When I saw her, I was struck by her appearance, feeling as though she resembled an angel. They had a long conversation with me, explaining everything in detail and trying to make me feel better about their proposal. Comforted by her presence, I tentatively agreed to go with them.

9
NEW FAMILY

About three days after the pastor and his wife visited, they returned to the rural yard where I lived to take me away. Before I left, I asked the lady I was staying with if I could come back if they threw me out. I wanted to ensure I had somewhere to go if things didn't work out. Given my past experiences, I had little reason to believe this new situation would be any different. Despite hearing all they said, I couldn't bring myself to trust them. I felt undeserving of the love and family they offered, convinced I would have to fight for my place, either physically or for food. The prospect of having a father and mother was alien to me, and I was unsure of what would be expected of me in this new environment. These people didn't know the challenges I carried with me—I felt like a burden, unworthy of their affection. How could they love me when I couldn't even love myself? I feared their intentions, wondering if they only wanted a maid or someone to serve them.

Leaving my friends behind was wrenching. They were the first true friends I'd ever had—girls who accepted me without judgment. We were close in age, with just a month between us, and I cherished our bond. The thought of being separated from them was agonizing. However, the pastor's wife reassured me that I could still visit my friend, offering me some solace amid the uncertainty. Grateful for this assurance, I left with mixed emotions.

As we prepared to leave, the pastor's wife surprised me by saying I wouldn't need my bags. She promised to take me shopping and buy whatever I wanted—clothes, shoes, school supplies. Skeptical, I brought my bags along anyway. Upon arriving at their home, she showed me a room she said was mine. I balked, unable to imagine having a space of my own without fear of punishment. She assured me things would be different now and that I could make the room my own, as long as I kept it tidy. In the evening, they took me shopping, allowing me to choose items in any color I liked. Despite my happiness, I couldn't shake the feeling of unease, as if I were waiting for the other shoe to drop.

By this time, I was about 12 years old and had started high school early. Despite my tumultuous emotions, I excelled academically and was respected as the class prefect for my school. I lived with my new parents for about a year, but I struggled to let them love me. I remained closed off, unable to reciprocate their affection, consumed by bitterness and anger. I had grown accustomed to being alone and doubted whether I even wanted love anymore. Despite the comfort of my new surroundings, I remained guarded, expecting things to change at any moment—after all, trouble seemed to follow me wherever I went.

10

LEGAL ADOPTION

By the time I was legally adopted, I had already lived in about nine or ten different homes with people. I still visited the girls at times, but I made sure not to overstay my welcome. I learned to pay attention when people were growing tired of me. Soon, I noticed a change in the family dynamic. The man and his wife decided they wanted to legally adopt me and asked me to call them Mom and Dad. I couldn't understand why they would want to do that. They didn't know the kind of damage I could cause, nor did they understand that I didn't deserve to be loved. I didn't want to hurt their family or cause them any pain. They said they wanted me to be with them forever, to be their daughter as if they had given birth to me. I tried to explain my true story to them, expressing my fear of not being able to love them and my anxiety about causing problems. I even asked them to send me back to my friend's house to avoid any trouble. Despite their kindness, I couldn't shake the feeling that they didn't truly love me and were trying to deceive me.

Living with them brought many changes. They provided me with my own room, adorned with pretty blankets and a window, and even a bathroom that we cleaned together—a new experience for me. Most mornings, she made breakfast for me, and sometimes she taught me how to cook. I was okay with learning these tasks, as with my aunts, I had to figure everything out on my own. However, things took a strange turn when she started saying things like she loved me and cared about me. These words frightened me because I couldn't believe them to be true. I became nervous and scared around them all the time. They encouraged me to talk to them during dinner, asking about my day and how I felt. They wanted me to smile, but I felt I had no reason to.

When the day came to go to the courthouse for the legal adoption, I was 13 years old and had been living with them for about a year. Despite living as a family, I had never called them Mom or Dad. They tried to prepare me for the judge's questions, but I wasn't ready. When we arrived, the pastor's wife couldn't join us, leaving me puzzled. We discovered we didn't have all the necessary documents, and one required a biological parent's signature. The pastor searched for my parents and found my mother through my aunt, who then signed the papers. Although the pastor was ecstatic, I felt devastated, believing my own mother had discarded me. The next day, we returned to the courthouse, and I was asked if I wanted to keep my first name and middle name. I chose to keep my first name but changed my middle name to Deborah, feeling it symbolized a new beginning. My new parents signed the documents, and I became their daughter. Overwhelmed with emotion, I cried like a baby, realizing I now had my very own parents and a new life ahead, learning how to be their daughter.

II
THE JOURNEY

The journey began with my new family, learning from each other and growing together as a family. It was okay at first; the pastor's wife and my new adoptive mother, she worked really hard on trying to teach me to love myself. She wanted to give me permission to smile if I felt like smiling or to cry if I felt like crying. She wanted me to know that it was okay to call her mom and that she would love me no matter what. She wanted to teach me everything, like how to be a young lady and respect myself and others. She taught me how to cook and clean properly and how to take care of my clothing and my other feminine hygiene situations. She helped me get ready for school each day and waited for me in the evenings as I came home.

After a little while, things began to change. I accepted that there was my mom and dad, and not much convincing, they won the battle; I now called them Mom and Dad. That was a big milestone for me because it meant that I trusted them and that I was learning how to love them and that I was letting them love me. I lived a little walking distance from the bus stop to the house, but on my way to and from school, I always had to pass my dad's office where he worked.

As soon as I got off the bus, I would go to the office to say hi to my dad and to let them know I was off the bus safely and I was heading to Dad's office to do my work and then on my way home to Mom. One day, I stopped by the office to say the usual to my dad: hi dad, I'm off the bus safely, and I'm heading home to do my homework, then I expected to leave. But when I walked into the office, the secretary was not at the desk as usual. The place seemed a little empty, so I walked to my dad's office. As I approached, I heard laughter, and without thinking, I opened the door and was shocked. My dad was on top of the desk having sex with the secretary; I was right and scared, slammed the door, and ran. He came after me to calm me down and to explain. He made a lot of promises to me that night and begged me not to say anything. But of course, I would not because I probably would be blamed for it. I said nothing because I loved my dad, and I was afraid.

The next day, I tried to keep everything as normal as I could, so I stopped by the office again. This time, Dad insisted that I stay at the office with him because he was getting ready to leave, and we could go home together. All of that makes sense to me. After all, I got to walk home with Dad, and that made me feel very special and happy. As we walked home, we stopped and got ice cream, something I had never imagined could happen to me - something this good.

This happened two or three days out of one week, and then my mother began to complain. Because I would wait for Dad at the office, I would be late for dinner and be up late at night doing my homework, and Mom did not like that. So, they would get in arguments about me in that situation. I would think, "Now that the problems have started with me, I might as well start packing." I knew that all this was too good to be true and that I would eventually be a big issue in this.

He mentioned to her that he wanted me to stop at the office at least 2 to 3 days a week so that he could have his fatherly walk with me. Even though mom did not like it, she allowed it. She waited for us when she knew we were on our way home each night that I stayed at the office after school. Sometimes, I would do my homework while I waited for it so that I didn't have to do it when I got home, and I would pray that that would make my mom happy.

One particular evening, I did what I always did: go to the office to wait for Dad. This time, it was different. I walked into the office where I usually sat, which was kind of a lobby area, and I was fine because there was a table for me to do my homework. Dad called me into his office to talk to him because he had no meeting and there was no one else there, so I said okay. He asked me to sit in his lap, and I did. He started to rub my back and arm, and I was okay because that was my dad. As soon as I felt funny, I got up and returned to my seat. He noticed that I felt funny and asked me if I was okay; I said, "Dad?" He ignored that and asked me, "why did you move?" I smiled and said, "you ready to go home?" That same incident happened for a few days.

I wanted to share it with my mom, but I was extremely scared because I did not want to get a beating or given a punishment for saying I was uncomfortable. After getting home one evening from the office, I was asleep in my bedroom when I could feel someone's hand under my blanket in my private area. I jumped to notice that it was my dad. He said that he was just fixing my sheet and making sure I was okay, then he sat on my bed and began to talk and put his hand on my stomach. I immediately began to move off the bed because I was terrified. All of my past came rushing through my mind like a hurricane to the ocean floor. I was very uncomfortable. I attempted to call for Mom, so he got up and slowly walked out of the room. I was very quiet the next morning and scared.

I knew this was too good to be true. There was no way this was real, and I was right. There I go again. I am making this man touch me because I am here in his home, and I should not be here. This is my fault. The next night, he came again, and put his hand in my panties and began to rub until I cried. I felt helpless and afraid, but I did not want to scream because I was afraid of a beating. After he left the room, I waited until I knew he was resting in the other room, and I packed a bag and left the house. It was late so I did not know where to go I went in the back of the yard and sat under an almond tree behind some sheets hanging on the clothesline in front of it.

I sat there until daylight. I could hear my mother frantically looking for me, but I just cried. I felt dead, and I did not want to show my face; I wanted to snap my finger and disappear. Eventually, she saw me in the backyard and came back there to get me and asked me why am I outside with my backpack. I just cried and told her I was afraid but I didn't want to wake her up that maybe I should not be there. I just told her I didn't like the house, and I was uncomfortable, and I wanted to know if I was going to get a beating from leaving the house. She said no and that we would talk about it later.

I did not go to school that day; Mom allowed me to stay home so that she could try to figure out what was wrong with me. I did not say a word about what happened because I knew I would be called a liar and one whom I could get beaten and thrown out. He did not come back into my room for a few days. then, one day, we had a family meeting when my dad came home. They were very excited to give me the news that we would move out of the country and that I would start going to school there. I was very happy and thought that maybe this would give all of us a fresh start and I could meet new people and things could be better.

Mom, Dad, and I -- the three of us moving away was very exciting, and I could not wait to fly on the plane for the first time. This news gave me a little hope for a while, and it felt good. Mom and Dad were nice to each other, which was so nice to see. That same weekend, my Mom decided she wanted to go shopping for our trip. I wanted to go but could not go because I was not feeling well. My monthly cycle was on, and it made me feel weak. When Mom came home, I was asleep in bed, so I didn't see what she had bought. It must have been a Sunday because I remember waking up to prepare for school. Dinner was already done when I got home from school that day, and she seemed excited to see me. She welcomed me with lots of love and smiles. She told me that she had a surprise for me and that I should change out of my school clothes so that she could talk to me about something. She asked me to meet her in her bedroom because what she wanted to say was very private. I was so excited that I got to have a special talk with my new Mom.

She started to take clothing from the bag and explained each item and the reason for buying them. I was in total terror as she explained that each piece was a sexual attraction to men and how they should be worn. I was in disbelief at what was happening. She began to tell me stories of how my dad had been sleeping with other women and say that's the reason why he was always taking so long to come home in the evenings. She said she loves him very much and we should make him happy by wearing some of these for him. She explained that he likes younger women and that she knows that he would like what we were planning for him. I immediately started to cry and say that I was afraid, but she assured me strongly that this would be okay and that it would be our family secret. I quivered in total confusion and shock at what my mom was asking me to do. Dad came home that evening, and I went to hide in my room. Mom welcomed him home with smiles and open arms. As I listened, she told him that we had a nice surprise for him. He was unsure what was happening, so he kept asking her what was happening, but she said nothing.

What's going on? he asked, but she smiled. She came to my room and told me to listen to her call and ask me to come into her room when they were ready. I waited for about 20 minutes, then she called. I went to the door and just opened it to enter, just like she told me to do. When I looked, I saw my mom on her knees; you can imagine the rest. I jumped and attempted to leave, but I was told to come in and close the door. He seemed shocked and asked her what she was doing but she persisted and kept on. She spoke a little and said, we both spoke and agreed that we wanted to do something nice for you because we love you, but he was a little confused, at least so it seemed, as he continued to allow this to go on. Now she was ready for me to have a turn and I was shaking.

I thought the earth was going to open up and swallow me. I have got to be dreaming; there is no way that this is really happening in real life. This was real, and I couldn't believe it. I started feeling very weak and nauseated and wanted to vomit; I got very sick and suddenly opened the door and ran out, still dressed in one of the outfits that she bought for me to wear. She came out after me, covered me with a sheet, and told me to go ahead into my room. That night, I cried myself to sleep. The day came for us to go to the airport to fly away, and it was just Dad and me. I did not understand what was happening, so I asked Dad where Mom was. He told me that she had a few meetings that had to be done in a city and that she would be up shortly, maybe in about a week or two. He said we would be staying with my aunt, his sister, until mom came up, then we could get her own place; I said great. My aunt had other children around my age and maybe a little older. I was so happy because I would have other people around me besides my Dad.

While we were staying with my aunt, things got bad. We were all in the living room one night watching TV, and my Dad was on the couch. I was lying next to him on the floor, and my other two cousins were on the other side of the floor. We all fell asleep; it seemed like we were in front of the TV at the same time. I was startled by his fingers rubbing on my vagina when I slept, so I screamed and protested," what was going on?!!!"

He started to say that I was lying and grabbed me by the chest, put me up against the wall and began to slap my face and body. My cousins and my aunts were in shock, and they apparently didn't know what to do. They stood by for a little bit. As they watched him beat me, I could tell they were confused. My aunt grabbed him and pushed him away and started to ask me if I was ok. Terrified and scared, I shook my head and tried to explain what happened, and he lunged at me again, pushed her out of the way, and continued to punch and beat me. I managed to escape and try to run outside, and one of my cousins came out with me. That day, I thought I was going to die.

We were all up for the rest of the night. Scared and confused, I began planning to do something drastic to stop this from happening again. My dad and my aunt had a friend that was only a block away, and without telling the friend exactly what happened, they just let her know I needed somewhere to stay since my dad had to leave on business. The next day, I moved over to stay with the lady.

Not long after, maybe about two weeks, my dad came there as well. He said that Mom was on the way there that day and that she was going to come with us to the friend's house, so I did not have to be there by myself with him. I stayed in that house the entire day, waiting for Mom to arrive. That night, I asked if Mom was on the way, but I didn't get an answer.

I was lost for words. She was the one and only mom that I knew, I have managed to push her somehow away and ruin their family. I felt I just deserved to die; that was my thinking because I couldn't do this anymore, so I deserved to die.

That night, I went to the restroom, took two full bottles of whatever pills I could find in there, and tried to kill myself. Like everything else, I could not even do that right because I woke up the next morning in bed. I was lying on the bathroom floor when the lady found me and placed me on my bed. I was very upset with her because I didn't want to be there. When she was not paying attention, I tried to pack a bag so I could leave at night when she was asleep. When I woke up that morning, my dad came to my room and told me to pack my things. He said he had already withdrawn me from school, so I was good to go. He advised me that we were going to America.

12

TRAVEL TO CANADA AND AMERICA

It took us two days to drive from Canada to America because we stopped at hotels along the way. The whole two days of driving, I was fighting him off, trying to protect my body. By this point, I was 14, almost 15, and I was tired and drained—not from the trip, but from the constant struggle. We eventually arrived at our destination, a small house on the beach. It was beautiful. Again, I had high hopes that maybe this new place, new environment, and new people would allow me to leave behind the horrors of my past.

He promised me that he would do better, that he would never touch me again. He assured me that we would go to counseling and that I would start a new school. For a while, everything seemed okay, and I tried my best to stay strong. I started attending a local school, and everything was going well.

After about four months, he told me that we had to move and that we would be staying with a friend. After about 30 days, Dad asked the people if I could stay there for a while because he had to go back to his hometown to take care of some business. I ended up staying with them for about a year until my dad returned permanently. We eventually got a new home, and I kept attending the same school. I was doing well academically.

But then it started again. One night, while I was sleeping, he came into my room and tried to have sex with me. I said no repeatedly, but he became angry, saying he saved me from my past and had done a lot for me. He mentioned how he saved my life and took me out of poverty. I was upset and ready to fight him. I told him I would call the police. He threatened that if I did, I would be sent back home—a nightmare I couldn't bear. I begged him to stop, but he continued, claiming he deserved it. I cried and screamed, but nobody outside could hear me. He became extremely upset, grabbed me, threw me in the shower, turned the water on, and then beat me.

The next morning, he apologized and tried to be nice, but I got dressed and went to school. He took away a lot of things I liked. I had four games I enjoyed playing and a couple of girlfriends I would call on the house phone. He also stopped giving me lunch money for school, so I went days without eating. He said he wouldn't do anything for me because I wouldn't do anything for him.

One day, I was sitting by the cafeteria, and my principal asked if I had any lunch. I said no, and he took me to the lunchroom and signed me up for free or reduced lunch. I was so happy—he was my savior that day because I felt weak and drained from hunger.

After about two weeks, I came home and noticed a strange car in the driveway. I walked up to the house, put my keys in the door, and opened it as usual. I couldn't believe my eyes! The secretary from the office was sitting in our living room with my dad, cuddling. I walked in and spoke to my dad, asking how his day was. He answered and asked about mine. I explained my day and classes and said everything was good. I began to walk toward the kitchen to do my homework when my dad asked, "Don't you see someone else in the room?" I said, "Oh hey!" with an attitude. She said she didn't want my hello because it was nasty.

I asked why she was there and told her she couldn't stay. My dad and the woman got angry, and we began to yell and fight. It was uncomfortable for everyone, and I asked my dad if I could stay with a friend. He said yes. I called a friend, and her mother said I could stay there for the night. I ended up staying for about a week, waiting for the woman to leave. One day, my dad came to see me and told me she wasn't leaving because she was going to become his new wife. He explained that she would be going back home for a few months to organize things before coming back permanently. I was very sad and felt like I was losing my dad, the only person I had in my corner.

It was bittersweet because I thought maybe he wouldn't want to touch me anymore since she was around. However, I didn't like her because I didn't know her true intentions. Since the first time I met her, I heard a lot of bad sexual things about her, so I didn't want Dad to get hurt. Dad always tried to defend her and make excuses for her, but she had a bad reputation. I was confused and frustrated. He also said his divorce from my mom was final and that she had gotten pregnant by someone else, so they weren't going to work anyway.

He asked me to come back home while she was gone. By this point, it was my last year in high school, and I had decisions to make before she returned. I went back to Dad until I could figure out what to do. He didn't try anything sexual with me during this time. I became very active in school and involved in programs to keep my mind off home life. I joined a church in the area and found a supportive youth group. I became strong in the church and became the new dance director for the girls. That's when I found my first passion in ministry.

One night, I went home, and he told me she was coming back the next day. I had nowhere to go, so I was upset and didn't want her to come. My dad became angry and started beating me. That night, while he was sleeping, I packed a bag and ran away. I was afraid, walking down the street late at night with nowhere to go. I saw a big house on the beach with a high raised basement, so I crawled underneath and slept there. I was hungry, and when they threw away their trash from dinner, I took some to eat. The next day, I walked into a nearby restaurant and sat by the window with no money. I saw him walking the streets looking for me, so I hid.

When I knew he was gone, I grabbed my things and ran back to the house. I took a shower and sat in the car, waiting for him to come home. He asked where I was, and I told him I was just sitting on the beach. He became upset and punched me. Not long after, I was introduced to a young man by a friend. He was interested in me and wanted to date, but my dad wouldn't allow it. He said if I brought any boy into my life, he would kill me. I told him I was still going to date, and in anger, he said, "If I can't have you, no man can!" His behavior was scary and intimidating, and I didn't know what to do. He threw things at me and cursed me out. Then he told me to get over it because he wouldn't let it happen.

After a while, he realized I was still trying to date the guy, but by this point, the lady was back, occupying his mind—praise the Lord! One evening, the woman and I got into a fistfight, damaging a lot of things in the house. The cops were called by the neighbors, but no charges were filed. After much conversation, she began to tell him to let me date because it might be good for me. I didn't like her speaking up for me because I thought she was trying to get rid of me.

One afternoon, he asked me about the young man. I told him I liked him and wanted him to meet my friend. To my surprise, the meeting went well. Dad behaved, and the young man was okay. I was shocked but terrified the whole time, hoping my dad wouldn't say anything crazy. He didn't. I continued attending the local church, where I met a woman who felt like a mother to me. Despite my experiences, I felt a strong motherly pull from her. She took in homeless girls, so I asked if I could live with her and the other girls, and she said yes. I explained my situation to her.

I went back home and told my dad I couldn't live with him and the woman. I told him my friend's mother said I could stay with her. He wanted to speak with her to ensure I would be properly supervised. She assured him it was a good Christian environment. He seemed to want to make sure she would take care of me until I graduated from high school. During this time, my relationship with the young man grew stronger. I'll tell you more about that in the chapters ahead.

13

THE BEGINNING OF THE NEW JOURNEY

With loving arms, I was welcomed into this new family of young girls by one of the ministers of the church I was attending. Within the first few months, I realized that I was a natural-born leader. All the girls were around the same age as me and came from broken homes, with no family nearby. We were all part of the church's dance ministry and lived together for about four years. During my time there, I became the leader of the group, ensuring the house was clean and tidy, and that everyone respected the home we were blessed to live in. Even at a young age, the girls came to me for counseling. I seemed to be the one they trusted, always giving them advice, so they kept coming to me.

I made sure all the bathrooms were clean, the living area was tidy, and the kitchen was properly maintained for meal preparation. I seemed to be the only one strong enough to prevent constant fighting and arguing. Looking back, I realize I was the voice of reason for the girls, despite all my own problems.

The lady I stayed with became like a mother to me, and her husband became like a father. There were many times when they would argue, like any married couple. Sometimes, when she was upset, I would talk to her and try to comfort her, making her feel better about their fights because I was so grateful for her help. Somehow, I made her feel better, and when he returned, they would rekindle their marriage.

By this time, I had just turned 18 and was preparing to graduate from high school. I felt a sense of responsibility for all the girls in the house, and they respected me as if I were the elder, though I was not. All I could think about was what would happen to me after graduation. I had signed up for volunteer hours at the hospital, hoping to get a job there once I graduated. In the meantime, I kept in touch with my adoptive dad, who promised to buy me a car as soon as I graduated.

One day, we went to a car lot to pick out the car I wanted. He gave me high hopes, saying, "As soon as you graduate, we'll buy this car. I'm saving for it." I was so excited that I worked hard to get all my credits to graduate and applied for a job at the hospital. I was thrilled about starting my new life with the car.

Graduation day came, and I was extremely excited. I was looking for my dad but couldn't find him at first. As I crossed the stage, I saw him standing at the entrance of the building. I was so happy, thinking we were going to get my car. I hoped that our father-daughter relationship could improve from here. After turning my tassel and graduating, I rushed to him and told all my friends that I was going with my dad to get my car.

I hugged him, and he said he was proud of me. However, he began to explain that he was short on the money needed to buy the car. He asked for some more time and promised he would still get it for me. I told him I understood and gave him a big hug. He said he had to go.

The next time I saw him was about two weeks later at a store. His new wife was driving the exact same car I wanted, and I was devastated. After that day, I didn't see him again for about two years. When I finally saw him in a store, I was already married and pregnant with my first son.

14

KEEP IT PUSHING

I had just graduated high school and was trying to find my way as a young adult. Without a car, I couldn't go very far to do the things I needed to do, so I walked everywhere, which was good for me anyway. By the time I graduated, I was still dating the young man. I joined the ministry and helped start a dance group in the church. I decided that I wanted to go back to school, so I registered at the local community college with the goal of earning a degree in business management. I stayed there for almost two years but could not graduate due to financial reasons. I decided to work full-time in the ministry with the leaders there and continued to help young girls as they needed assistance finding education, jobs, and such.

I became very passionate about my youth program at the church and began traveling with the group to dance at various events. I really enjoyed it. I didn't need much because I was satisfied with how things were. I just wanted to survive and become the best that I could be. I didn't have any money, family, or anyone to assist me with further advancement. Even though I was one of the teenagers living in the home with other teenagers, I was more like a mother to them all. As mentioned before, I carried myself in a way that commanded respect. Many days, I walked with confidence as if I were well-educated and financially set. I began to set values for myself and held my head up high. I started to create a plan for where I wanted to go in the future. In the middle of it all, I was still dating the young man, but we were not very serious yet.

Since all the girls looked up to me, there was no room for me to show my weaknesses. I had to stay strong and positive through my pain of loneliness and bitterness that I had gained through my life. Even though I had been dating him for months, it was all for show because I truly did not know how to love, and I didn't even love myself. It's amazing how we can live a fake life in front of everyone and give them the wrong impression that everything is alright. Somehow, even in my weaknesses, I knew how to be strong for others way back in those days.

One day, my pain overtook me. I needed someone to talk to, but there was no one I could talk to because everyone talked to me. There was no one to cry to because everyone cried to me. There was no one to lean on because it seemed like everyone leaned on me. There was no one to trust because it seemed like everyone wanted to trust me. I had so many things in my past that never got resolved, but as long as I was still breathing, life went on. After a while, some of the things from my past became overwhelming. So many things from my past haunted me like ghosts. The more I ran, the more they found me. I wanted to scream out loud to everyone because I was confused and lost. I just wanted to know what people saw in me that I couldn't see in myself. I wanted to tell them that I could not help them with their situations. They looked up to me so much. I knew what it was like to need a friend and a shoulder to cry on, to tell them how I really felt. I knew how it felt to want to be rescued and delivered from yourself.

Most days, I would frighten myself when I looked in the mirror. The way I perceived myself was different from the way I looked. How could someone who looked like me go through the things I was going through, none of which were my fault? This couldn't be true. As I counseled these young ladies about their anger, bitterness, pain, and frustration, I noticed one thing: each one of these girls carried a portion of my pain. I felt obligated to be there for them, though I didn't know why. I felt a responsibility to take care of people who had been hurt, even though I had been hurt. I have always heard that "hurt people hurt people," but I don't know if that statement is true. Despite all the pain, hurt, and rejection I've been through, it has caused me to become more compassionate and understanding toward others who are hurting. Now that I am dating as a young adult, I am trying to make sense of it all.

15
WHERE DO I GO FROM HERE?

I had gone through many changes since as far back as I could remember. By this point, I had just turned 19 and was wondering where I was going to live. I had to leave college because I did not have the money, and there was nobody around to advise me financially. I wasn't even aware that financial aid existed for students.

I had to sit down and think about where I wanted to go from there. I didn't want to stay in that house forever. I wanted to have my own house someday. Wow, what am I thinking? I will never buy a house, I will never have enough money, I'm so ugly no one would want to be with me anyway. These were some of the things my aunt used to say, so I started to believe them. Why didn't I just kill myself when I was younger? I wouldn't have to worry about these new things if I had. This guy that I'm dating probably just wants what everyone else wanted, and then he'll be gone. Maybe I am good for nothing just like my aunt said. I will never have children, and even if I do, I hope I never have a girl. I do not want any other girl to go through what I have been through. These were my thoughts at age 19. I couldn't believe I had lived to see this age. I believed I was just going to handle it because if I had to continue to fight for myself for the rest of my life, I wouldn't win. These were my thoughts at the time.

At that moment, I decided to go down to the beach. Knowing that I couldn't swim, I decided I was going to walk into the middle of the water until I sank to the bottom. I believed that was the best thing for me and the world. Yes, I knew I was helping others, and it was a great thing, but I needed someone to help me, and I had no one. I was lost in the words that were spoken to me: that I would be nothing, that I was a liar, that I was good for nothing, and that I would become nothing. I was so skinny with nappy hair, big breasts that I hated with a passion, and I did not like the mole on my lip. For the third or fourth time, I decided to end it all, and again I failed. I was getting ready to walk into the water, and I was in the water up to my knees. Suddenly, a little ball came bouncing my way, and I heard a little child asking me to catch it for her. The child yelled out to me, "Hey! Can you please bring me that ball back?" I pretended that I didn't hear, but the child insisted, "Can you please throw me the ball?" she asked. I became very annoyed because I really wanted to get this over with, and here came this kid wanting me to catch a ball I cared nothing about. Out of frustration, I turned around to reach for the ball. When I attempted to throw it to her, she was too far away. I had to get out of the water to bring the ball to her because it was also windy.

She was so happy that I brought her the ball. She asked me if I could play with her, so I looked around to see if anyone was watching. I just wanted to be mean and tell her to go away. When I looked up to my right, I saw her parents watching to see what I would do. As the little girl was asking me to play with her, I felt really bad, so I played with her until I was tired. I decided I was going back to the house to get some rest. I felt extremely tired and weak. As I tried to walk away from the water, I kept sinking as if it wanted to pull me in by its strength. For a moment, I became a little afraid that I would not be able to get out of the water. It felt like quicksand. Every time the water came up toward the shore, it felt like it was trying to pull me away. Every step I took toward dry land, the sand was sinking under my feet, trying to make me stay in the water. Suddenly, I felt even more in control of my life and decided that if I was going to die, I wanted to do it my way, and this sand would not do it for me.

I went back to the house that evening, fixed myself something to eat, then took a shower before going to bed. That night, for some reason, all the girls gathered in my room and sat beside my bed to thank me for helping them. They also let me know that their lives had not been the same since I came there. Two of the girls had a dispute and were waiting for me to get home so that I could help them resolve their problem. The adults of the home were there. Why didn't they go to them for help? This is when I noticed that there was something very different about me and my peers. I couldn't put my finger on it, but I just knew I was different. I just had to figure out what the difference was and how to tap into it. I began to think about all I'd been through and looked at all the people that depended on me to help them through their problems. All I could think of was that there had to be something or someone out there in the heavens that was looking out for me. I suddenly felt special and started to think that I'd been chosen.

From this point forward, I realized that out of all the people in the world, I must've been chosen for a special reason. I started to try to find some positive things about myself to see if I had any. To see if I had any good values and to see what I could create on my own. With this book, I have so much more to tell you.

As the story continues, you will realize that with all the hairs on your head, God knows and created each one. Each one is special in a unique way. God knows your DNA for every single strand. GOD PLACED me in this big world and singled me out from among the rest. He chose me out of all my peers and all of my family, and that makes me THE SPECIAL STRAND.

DON'T STOP READING, IT'S NOT OVER UNTIL IT'S OVER.

ABOUT THE AUTHOR

Dr. Amoy D. Baker Ph.D. is a woman with a passion for reaching the world one person at a time. A native of Jamaica, Dr. Baker moved to Canada in 1990 with her missionary parents. At 15, her family relocated to America to establish a local church as part of their missionary work.

Dr. Baker attended high school and college in the United States, following in her parents' footsteps by becoming a pastor and counselor for her local church. She is the founder of Faith in Action Worship Ministries International, Community Empowerment and Support Inc., Faith in Action Bible College in Garner, NC, and Family Talk Christian Counseling.

Dr. Baker and her husband, Louis Baker IV, live in North Carolina and have three sons and four grandsons. Her foundational scripture is Philippians 4:13: "I can do all things through Christ, who strengthens me."

www.ingramcontent.com/pod-product-compliance
Lightning Source LLC
Chambersburg PA
CBHW030533080526
44586CB00011B/422